YOU KEPT YOUR SECRETS

poems by

Helen Marie Casey

Finishing Line Press
Georgetown, Kentucky

YOU KEPT
YOUR SECRETS

Copyright © 2020 by Helen Marie Casey
ISBN 978-1-64662-370-9 First Edition
All rights reserved under International and Pan-American Copyright Conventions. No part of this book may be reproduced in any manner whatsoever without written permission from the publisher, except in the case of brief quotations embodied in critical articles and reviews.

ACKNOWLEDGMENTS

And So I Watch ~ *Hawk & Whippoorwill*
Aviator ~ *Sweet: A Literary Confection*
Hopeful as Sky ~ *The Comstock Review*
It Happens at Laurelhurst Park ~ *Paterson Literary Review*
Language of Grief ~ *The Comstock Review*
Near the Edge of the Pond ~ *Paths, Tracks, Trails: Plein Air Poetry 2018*
The First Christmas ~ *Peauxdunque Review*
The Hawk and His Prey ~ *The Greensboro Review*
Winter Hawk ~ *Louisiana Literature*
You Kept Your Secrets ~ *Rock & Sling*
Your Tree ~ *Peauxdunque Review*

Publisher: Leah Huete de Maines
Editor: Christen Kincaid
Cover Art: Anita Kurth
Author Photo: Dean Casey
Cover Design: Elizabeth Maines McCleavy

Order online: www.finishinglinepress.com
also available on amazon.com

Author inquiries and mail orders:
Finishing Line Press
P. O. Box 1626
Georgetown, Kentucky 40324
U. S. A.

Table of Contents

Preface: The Hawk and His Prey xi
You Kept Your Secrets 1
The White Butterfly 2
There Is No Good Time to Die 3
Red-tailed Hawk 4
Red Rover, Red Rover, Come Over 5
Near the Edge of the Pond 6
Dance of Wind and Rivers 7
It Happens at Laurelhurst Park 8
Hopeful as Sky 9
When the Woodchuck 10
Dear Josh 11
Aviator 12
And So I Watch 13
All We Have 14
After You Die 15
Absent 16
Missing 17
Birthdays 18
Opting Out 19
The Language of Grief 20
No One Is Here 21
We Have Been Here 23
That Lone Hawk 24
The Coldest Month 25
Reappearance 26
Your Tree 27
April Brings Them Back 28
Winter Hawk 29

In Memory of Joshua Dean

PREFACE: The Hawk and His Prey

The hawk, still and waiting on a cold December day, is nearly as bleak as the winter landscape and patient, the way we are not. He does not move until he sights in, his prey unaware, unready. The field does not care, one way or the other, about the hawk and his prey. It is cold and if the field could speak words, I think they would be spare. What would there be to tell beyond the fact of falling temperatures, rising winds, and the need to hang on, regardless. Still and waiting, the hawk is almost prophetic. *One waits.* Sometimes that is enough. Sometimes that is everything there is.

You Kept Your Secrets

You kept your secrets, what there was
of darkness, concealed and trapped, yours alone.
Now your body is not your body. You left it hanging
on a branch, not one breath more for anyone.
We're trying to bring him back. I knew then
that you wouldn't return. We followed your inert body,
you in an ambulance, we riding in a police car. I think
there was no siren. Why would there be?

I don't remember much of that day. I know this:
we sat beside your stillness, touched and talked
to you. Six hours or more we sat with you.
We didn't want to leave you, the morgue
waiting, all of us thinking it too grim a place
for a boy like you, some stubble on your chin,
you still in braces, so near to having them off,
perhaps a new smile emerging when the wires
were gone. A priest came and went. Came
and went. I think he blessed you. Maybe
more than once he blessed you with oils.

Once, I imagined a small bird there on my windowsill
was you looking in. He had a bit of food in his mouth.
It made me happy to see you, to know that you are free
enough to fly, to come back to visit, however briefly.

The White Butterfly

Not much laughter this wormy day, chipmunks oblivious
to everything but their own running, their burrows, and we absent,
except to grief, not wishing for anything but mindless joy,
hands cupped for sorrows that will surely come hobbling
toward us. The white butterfly whose name I do not know
passes, of no more moment than Icarus's silent fall. How much
of what we have lost returns? How much is less than ash
under foot? Who can say what else the empty spaces might have held?

There Is No Good Time to Die

The swamp maple's dying begins at the top, leaves
drying into gold, vermilion, chartreuse before they drop,
mere clutter underfoot. Cold grows relentless,
like sorrow. After death, the wind does not matter.
Nothing matters except what is left, scraps
of memory, none of them hanging around, all of them
puzzle pieces, the code wrong, sky green, grass grey,
a face where ears should be, the bed empty, sheets missing.
There is no good time to die. Everyone asks about return,
whether, sometimes, a shadow passes, or sits a while.
I am afraid to look, afraid there will be nothing, everywhere.

Red-tailed Hawk

Windshield waiting, the red-tailed hawk struck and died,
a great mangled heap, feathered corpus deprived
of beauty, speed, insight. Windshield shattered. Driver
bereft, acceptable explanations invisible, as they often are.
Other scenarios too late to matter. Inarticulate narrator seeks
the threads of continuity, breach of continuity, motivation,
perhaps a theme. What good are tears when the rationale
is lacking, sky-diver missing his mark, mutilating himself?
Contrary to storied flights of windhovers, falcons, eagles.
Even crows know better. How often does their compass fail,
their sense of place and speed and timing awry?

Do you remember, dear boy, how we watched the ducks
and geese at Hager Pond, how we fed dried bread crusts
to them ? Each one insisted, "Me first." You flung your crust
to the sad-looking goose. Another stepped in front. Is this
what they call *Survival of the fittest?* Is this where nature
deceives us, the signals for fight instead of flight not strong
enough in you? Is this where the terminally-wounded bird
in our story causes my brother to wonder, are you now that
red-tailed hawk inert on the windshield, your destination
a miscalculation of unfathomable proportions?

In the end, I wonder if you saw all of them, the more than
two hundred kids, teachers, co-workers, friends, family,
who came to say "Good-bye" to you, to tell you how much
they loved you, before you disappeared from view, locked in
another existence where, we are meant to assume, no pain
punctuates the landscape, where no trees wait for you,
no branch holds you above the ground, no arms gather you.

Red Rover, Red Rover, Come Over

The year decides to run away from us, a game
of tag we shall lose. Clocks outrun us, time
a fleet-foot Cinderella. No one will come knocking
at the door, a slipper of years returned to us.
Waves take us where we do not want to go,
an undertow of losses until some mermaid calls,
the fog gathers, and we become seabirds
who can no longer fly. The world does not care.
We map where we have been, become Sherlock,
want to know where we are going, then the going
gets lost. There is no end we like, scarlet questions
unanswered, decline the one sure thing. The barge is filled
with coins no longer current. Of course they will not
pay our way. We will be sent back, the gatekeepers unrelenting.
We will not know anything more than we now know except
to trudge on, thrusting our bodies against hands that hold fast.

Near the Edge of the Pond

Two moths dance as you disappear,
the trail winding through pines, oaks,
maples, reeds by the shore, and lily pads.
I decide not to call out to you, not to
disturb you in this tranquil place.
It is enough to converse with trees,
enough to watch for trout leaping,
wild rhododendron, acorn caps, fields
of fern. Pond scum and pine cones grow
content to be here, clouds keeping
what they know to themselves, not
unlike the blackbird, not unlike
the plane high overhead, a vessel
of secrets inclined toward the sun.

Diaphanous wings of the dragonfly
overshadowed, one Great Blue Heron
lifts above the ceiling of trees, almost
leaving a shadow of spun charcoal ink.
Seeing what is and what isn't here,
I think of you, of how you would have
liked discovering the bear poop,
turkey droppings, fallen feathers,
nests, fingerlings, and stones that look
a little like arrowheads. You are,
at the same time, not here and yet,
you are everywhere, almost the way
the large and small fish in the pond
are here even when I can't see them
beneath the still, still surface, beneath
the dark, impenetrable waters.

Dance of Wind and Rivers

Raven. Chinook. Steelhead. Snowberry. Sage.
What do we become when we cease to be
who we were? Heart of the black bear, branches
crushed under foot, how do we learn to dance
with wind? Our shadow seeks the shadows of all
we love. Fox follows our steps. Lightly. Lightly.
Alder. Cedar. Fir. Mighty Sequoia. Birch.

How much do we hear when we are called
by name, when we pray and there is barely
a whispered response hanging somewhere
in the air? The Long Tom listens, flows on, sun
riding the ripples, spirits of the Kalapuya,
beside the banks, enigmatic as night song.
Gray wolf. Bobcat. Bald eagle. Rattlers.

It Happens at Laurelhurst Park

It is not a large pond. Nothing about it disturbs
the afternoon or, at least, not at first. Nothing
is out of joint. Ducks swim. Boys watch. Sunshine
beats down on grass beside the pond. Water ripples.
As if it is a prank, one duck pushes down the head
of another, and then, as if by signal, all the ducks
swarm. The attackers peck the top of his head,
plucking his feathers until they lay bare a circular
area. They continue to push that single duck under
water. Not one tries to help the drowning duck.
The boys who watch begin to fidget. They throw
stones to stop the attack. The youngest boy cannot
stand it. In he goes to save the injured one. He puts
his arms around the creature. He cradles the duck
to the pond's edge. The boys kneel around the body.
They regret waiting too long. If they had understood,
they would have saved him. They're sure they would.

Hopeful as Sky

Blue fights through and sky loses face, goes nondescript,
becomes a roof of gun metal, sightless above Sudbury.
A bully woodpecker probes the highest limb. Behind him
crows scavenge for sustenance. We all chase after what
we need, predators of something, someone. Insatiable.
We all fight through. We all ride currents, waters murky
before the dive begins, before we know what we do not know,
before we give ourselves, wide open and hopeful as sky
before the hush, before the final soft sift of silence.

When the Woodchuck

Acorns and squirrels skydive, trees russet-leaved, and I watch.
Here, where I am, I can no longer find you among the oaks or maples, pines waiting, not even when the woodchuck devours the coneflowers, nor as the turkeys do their funny trot down the long, potholed driveway, not when the lights go out. Yet, in the darkness, I listen for you.
There is a melancholy logic in the question, *Are you searching, too?* but I don't think so. Wouldn't I know if your spirit had returned? Woudn't I know if you were scouting in the woods for deer or squirrels? If you tried to call a greeting of one kind or another? The camouflages you liked to test are working this time. No one can keep you in sight, and not one of us knows the secret code. By design, much more slowly than we ever thought possible, we learn to appear almost content.

Dear Josh

Your brother, bereft, dreams that you decide
not to be dead any longer. He watches you
bend your left knee upward, slowly rise,
ready to lift yourself out of the dark box
where you are coffined, bored, restless.
He watches the effort you make deciding
where freedom lies. Inside? Outside?
Then you ease back and settle in.

How can he know if you wanted to
change your mind, the noose tightening,
winter coming on, the scarf you wore
killing you, a knot darkening your throat
into which medics will thread a tube,
a ventilator waiting to breathe for you.

Aviator

You make funny faces at the camera, clown-like boy
in flannel pajamas, a red toy car in your hands, maybe
eight years old and, for the moment, happy. We watch
the years pile on, you teaching your cousin, the one who
idolizes you, how to scale the highest backyard mountain,
the two of you, survivors, coming indoors for cookies and
milk. Before you destroyed it, you kept a journal. I wonder
what you confided, which kind of code you used, and if it
helped at all, before you decided there was no point. What
could spilling words onto a page do? Did you try to say it,
how desolate you felt, the loneliness growing too large
to encompass, the cold, hard struggle to clamber down
the cliff more than you could embrace until you decided
you'd had enough. You decided to unburden yourself.
Totally unburden yourself. You climbed up, you tied
your wool scarf, tested a bit, then tightened the knot,
as any aviator would, visibility cloudy, winds turbulent.

And So I Watch

Red-tailed hawks are said to have
excellent vision. Still, one crashed.
He killed himself on a car windshield.
How meaningful can that be?

You chose a tree, the same one
you began to climb when you were
just twelve, yearning to be bigger,
stronger, more muscled, and agile.

Now no one wants to look at the tree
because they keep seeing you, inert.
It's like looking at your Christmas gifts,
the ones you didn't live to open. Time

stopped. Altered. *Before.* Then *After.*
Nothing else except vacancy and
the scream of the red-tailed hawk
whose flight is notably deliberate.

The hawk occasionally hovers on beating
wings, and so I watch for you, thinking
you watch, too, but not all the time.
Not all the time.

All We Have

The moment we have is all we have.
We run, time always winning the game
of chase and remember.

Death manicures his nails,
listening to every fervid conversation,
minding his secrets.

We mind, too, knowing in every fiber this
will vanish, the bright balloon we call our life,
every breath slowly leaking away. We mind.

We are snowflakes lighter than angels
and more fragile. We mind the incessant questions
with no answers, sentences with no punctuation,
a few italics, the oddest script, which we cannot read.

And we do not know, we do not know,
flowers growing, the sun watching,
sky of rose-charcoal, tending its secrets.

After You Die

Your older brother keeps waiting
for your call and thinks you try,
but no one answers when he picks up.
He wants to know where you are.
He drives a limo and would come for you.
In a second, he would come for you.

It's the not knowing how to find you,
how to reach you, how to hear you,
that shreds him into incoherence,
as in *I can't hear you when you call.*
I'm waiting and I can't hear you. Please
call back. Please tell me where you are.

Do you want to take him by surprise,
jumping on him the way you did, years
gone by? Do you want to hide, the covers
dark and suffocating, the bedroom small,
the two of you making plans to fly away?
You'll bring a comforter, maybe a book,
toy soldiers, plastic aliens, your own pillow.

The measure of your height remains in place
on the wall, pencil mark after pencil mark,
your progress slowly steady before you knew
you couldn't wait for your brother, before you
gave up on toy soldiers, plastic aliens, pencil marks,
before you said, "What the hell?" and jumped.

Absent

You ask me what I used to have, and love,
no longer have, and miss. It's you I lack,
you I miss. You stood here, absent, even
to yourself, a thing mysterious as it is sad.
If there were ways to put you back together,
more whole than you have ever been, I would
begin the soldering but I cannot, cannot find
the way to know, do you want to be whole
or is there something dark you've learned to love
and cannot do without, something almost tangible
you long to put your arms around, to claim as better
than it was before, when all was Ivory bright?

Missing

You weren't here with your brother and your cousins,
you weren't here yesterday with your aunties, uncles,
parents, grandparents. You weren't here to celebrate
your birthday, a new school year, your wished-for-life
as a Marine. You weren't here to take your turn, you the
king of ice cream, scooping huge servings. You weren't here
except as absence, incredibly heavy absence, the one
everyone wanted to but couldn't touch, couldn't embrace
one more time, one more time. No one clowned around.
No one disappeared into the woods. No one went out
to chase deer or rabbits or hummingbirds. No one
wore your brand new combat boots or carried your
ratty briefcase. We missed your buzz-cut, the end
of your turn with braces, your silly jokes, the hugs you
tolerated, your teenaged appetite for burgers and chips.
Funny thing about absence, how real it is, how permanent.

Birthdays

Behind my back animals
eat the garden,
break the necks
of lilies,
chew in the dark.

I plant asters, yarrow, lilacs,
more lilies. I watch the garden
hesitate.

Impatiens grows beside the bleeding
hearts, black-eyed Susans nudge
snapdragons. Roses but no lilies.

Some fragrance. Some color. Some death.
That is the way of birthdays.

Opting Out

Your birthday is approaching but you've lost interest,
decided once and for all that being eighteen years old
is not all it's cut out to be, that you're opting out, no
birthday presents worth the effort, no cake enough
to keep you here, no words sufficiently strong; candles
balloons, and fanfare inadequate. What your needs are
you cannot say. Not even Christmas persuades you.
Santa is a fiction. The crèche figures are splintered
and dull. No games call your name.

Would it have mattered if we had held you tighter
or, would you have seen that as a prison? I want
to set a place for you and give you chores, hear you
laugh and share a silly pun. You told me once, as you held
a pet chicken in your arms, that you were going to be
an adventurer. I think you meant you would climb trees
as high as mountains, ford crocodile-infested waters, save
threatened kids in distant villages, and sleep in the open.
We hold your quilt now, your bed empty, the tree,
the one that killed you, desperate to have you back.

Language of Grief

They do not speak the language of grief,
these wind-wrapped trees. They do not keen
the losses, desiccation inevitable, endings
more necessary than beginnings. They live
otherwise, each moment its own journey,
the future a figment of alternate imaginations.
I am not like trees dropping their glory for winter.
Uncomplaining. I miss every leaf, every pine needle,
every limb that rots and drops. The scarlet ones
hold on and on, stubborn. The Japanese Maple
gives up everything at once. I shall insist on fighting,
the last gasp of color furious. Illuminating.

No One Is Here

I would visit you if I could, but you are not here
nor are you there, not anymore, which does not mean
that you are not because that is impossible, the very thought
of total absence abhorrent. Death has taken you and will not
give you back, except as memory, and memory will have to do,
a process: remembering and savoring the you we miss,
as in lack and want, as in grieve, as in *searching for*.

**

We don't even know about reunion except the reunion that comes
in dreams and wishes, though we want the coming together again
the way we first wanted love on earth, the absence of which makes life
nearly impossible. We work to keep love alive, a little like working
with every fiber to hold memory, which is constantly trying
to leak away from us, growing dim and misleading as walls do
in darkness, making us unsure unless we touch the dark
solidity we think we remember even as we reach around us,
touching a way of knowing, separate from theorizing, from wishing.

**

Others are also gone and I wonder: Do you meet with old friends there,
where you are, where we cannot see you or hear you, all of you hungry,
we imagine, for the old life. You are beyond the need for books,
but surely you miss them or, maybe not, what you now have so
indescribably good and sufficient. We imagine your return as something
you desire in the same way we do. When will you reach out? Will we
recognize you in your new invisibility, in your silence? Or will we
talk right past you, language no longer working to bridge the distance
between *now* and *not now*, between *present* and another kind of time,
a time outside of time, a kind of time for which we have no word, the
way we have no word beyond loneliness to tell the quantity of our loss,
insufficiency the name we give our being here, mired in time where you
are not, shadows everywhere, hovering the way shadows do, here and
gone.

✷✷

And what would I say, you in one chair, I in another, the specter of death present though he says not a word? He doesn't need to speak, of course, for he is holding your hand in his and even if I could see you, I know you don't fit here any more. You know what we don't. That makes all the difference, doesn't it? Knowing. It is not the same as believing. You know what is there on the other side, and you aren't saying. Is it because you can't or you won't? If you could, would we be sorry because it would mean the end of illusions, of hoping and pretending we will be permanently united, which is the point of wishing for you. Would you be telling us what we cannot bear? Have you become Ulysses, he who answered, "No one is here," when asked his name? Are you no one because you have become every one at the same time you are the "No one is here"?

✷✷

Your name is not the same as emptiness. It is worse. There is no way to summon you, to embrace you, to know you if you no longer own the name we knew. And if we call you, *Beloved*, would it make any difference at all? I touch the air you once breathed. I see the achingly beautiful, brilliant rose-colored azaleas you loved. The tiniest hummingbird enchants me as it once did you. You are here even when you are not. I watch while I am waiting. I am listening for the exhalation I will know.

We Have Been Here

Deep winter, snow erases signs
we have been here, stomping
our way. It doesn't matter that
we grope for handhold. Wind
matters and the blinding snow,
so white, so thick, it conceals
all edges, not like love, defining
everything it touches, brushstroke
certain, caress uncovering what
wants to be revealed. Night falls.
We disappear. And then the tongue
carves its own path through darkness,
light at the end of knowing, fragile act
of being. Snow dropping off the arms
of trees. Winter deep. Light erases
signs we have been here. Stomping.

That Lone Hawk

Am I wrong to think you have become that lone hawk, wrong to decide you love where you are, looking down on old neighborhoods you knew, no challenge so large you can't meet it? You know how to hunt, to slyly ferret around, how to swoop just in time for catch, no release.

Winter does not alarm you, the anniversary of your death transformed into a celebration of your wit and life. You wanted, you told us, *to be gray, to be invisible.* You didn't say you would be back, sailing the skies the way that trickster, Odysseus, sailed the seas, destroyed his enemies, returned.

The Coldest Month

Frigid weather. The kind of days that call most
significances into question, paring them down
to cold and hot with a long middle distance where
we pay almost no attention to what weather intends.
Winter asks no permission, rather like the owl
I listened to last night, three hoots, an interval, and
then he began again. What did he achieve, that interloper?
Did he roust a rodent as he interrupted the stillness?
Or, was it simpler? He sang the song he had been given.
He asked nothing more, neither meaning nor applause.
Unlike us, wanting, endlessly wanting, such simplicity
satisfied him. He will not change his habits tonight.
I will listen with fervor to his stolid, uncomplaining
refrains. I will fall asleep, listening across the iced
wind, across the moon's reflected light, across time's
slow hands, the face of time concealed, stealthy.

Reappearance

When I don't open my eyes, there you are, pretending you are invisible, your backpack light, your laughter almost audible, a joke on your tongue, something silly that takes your fancy. When you stocked shelves, you memorized every aisle, every ingredient, and tested yourself for accuracy. But you didn't last there. Easily bored. Off to another job, new challenges, the same old pattern: Not fun anymore. You tried wearing black, being invisible, and yet they knew you, those friends you brushed against. You threw away your new boots, the ones you sent for because they suited you. You tossed your trail of memories, what was left of toys, sketches, all signs you held a place here. There must have been a diary somewhere. It disappeared. Even your shadow stopped. You might have paused, but didn't. Christmas was coming. Let it, you must have said, and it did. You weren't here, or you were and chose to keep it a secret, your whereabouts.

Your Tree

Your tree is in bloom now. It unnerves us, the fact of it
persisting when you could not. Odd how so many ancients
survive and when they don't, even the verdant, lush idea
of what they became remains intact. The French are going to
rebuild Notre Dame to look as it used to, except newer. No one
wants changes we have to learn to love. We might have
grown to do without your tree, but who would have taken
the first cut? Who would have kept on knocking it down?
It's hard enough to find you now, except for this: We can't stop
talking to you. Thing is: We keep on listening for your response,
dry as it might have been, and ironic. I remember when you read
"Catcher in the Rye" and I didn't think you'd be able to relate,
Holden Caulfield so lonely and disconnected. In fact, you did.
You understood exactly the aloneness inside his loneliness,
the same way you got "Lord of the Flies" and "Animal Farm."
You didn't always know how to find your way home but you did
know—or maybe you thought you did—where the imagination could
take an active boy leading the pack in the dimmest, truculent turn.

April Brings Them Back

One scarlet cardinal returns, the oak begins to bud, and then
a squirrel rushes down, down to the scrub beneath the tree.
Overhead, a hawk pays no mind, his glide path clear, chipmunk
one more observer. Or not. April brings them back, God's creatures,
from wherever they have been. I pause to look, certain of this, buds
and shoots must want to be back or they wouldn't return, would they?
And you, do you ever want to un-do your decision to die in December—
the cold of winter vast and empty? Do you ever have the urge to chase
rabbits or squirrels one more time, to put your arm around a girlfriend,
to un-do the knot your winter scarf made, choking you to death?
Can you know how much we miss you, or is there a silence so serene
you have become like a kestrel, that small falcon that hovers before
he swoops, his prey helpless, the kestrel small as a dove but powerful,
more beautiful than a creature has a right to be. I have looked deep
into the eyes of a kestrel, touched his wings, the kestrel whose wing
was broken, and I have thought of you, flight interrupted. Grounded.

Winter Hawk

Would I were a winter hawk,
whited sedge, iced ponds, geese
in flocks below me, sky tufted,
grey squirrels climbing red oaks,
deer in the sodden fields, you,
young boy, hawk-like, spreading
your sweatered wings wide, joy-
filled shrieks slicing air the way
red-tailed hawks do, I diving,
mice running toward the marsh,
I swooping so near you, my
shadow would engulf you,
the way my arms once did.

Helen Marie Casey's chapbooks include *Zero Degrees, Fragrance Upon His Lips*, and *Inconsiderate Madness*, a finalist for the Julia Ward Howe Award of the Boston Authors Club. She has also written a biography, *My Dear Girl: The Art of Florence Hosmer*. In addition, she has written a monograph, "Portland's Compromise: The Colored School 1867-1872" and has won the Black River Chapbook competition of Black Lawrence Press, the 14th National Poet Hunt of *The MacGuffin*, and the Frank O'Hara Prize from *The Worcester Review*. Her work appears in several poetry journals, including, among many others, *The Laurel Review, Louisiana Literature, CT Review, The Worcester Review, Paterson Literary Review, Prairie Schooner, The Comstock Review, The Christian Century, Westchester Review, Peauxdunque Review, Greensboro Review,* and *The MacGuffin.*

www.ingramcontent.com/pod-product-compliance
Lightning Source LLC
LaVergne TN
LVHW041505070426
835507LV00012B/1340